MUST LOVE POETRY

CHRISELDA BARRETTO

Dedicated to my stars; Nikos, Christian and Melina

Love you to the moon and back!

CHRISELDA.BLOG

This is a work of creative nonfiction. Some parts have been fictionalized in varying degrees, for various purposes.

First Edition

ISBN 978-9-4638-8110-4 (paperback)

ISBN 978-9-4638-8111-1 (ebook)

D/2019/Chriselda Barretto, uitgever

Visit "chriselda.blog"

https://chriselda.blog/

Images by Canva

Table of Contents

MUST LOVE POETRY

 **Chriselda Barretto**

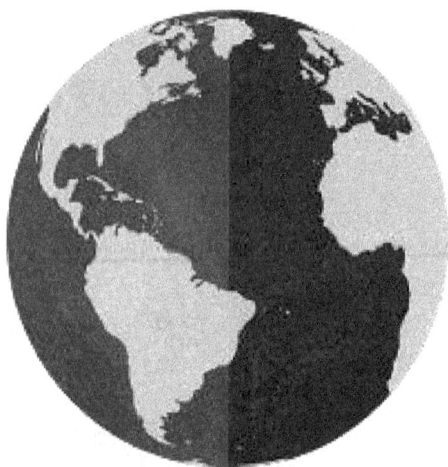

Tides Of Change

Long before you stepped foot here

Roamed you in another sphere

Walking it wasn't called then

Gliding smoothly from bend to bend!

This earth was not in existence

Easy it isn't forming this sentence

Evolution hitting from every side

To bring on a new, refreshing tide!

Fearful were we never for changes

What brought us here then they ask?

Dig deeper in your mind's eye

A fairly simple, gracious but important task!

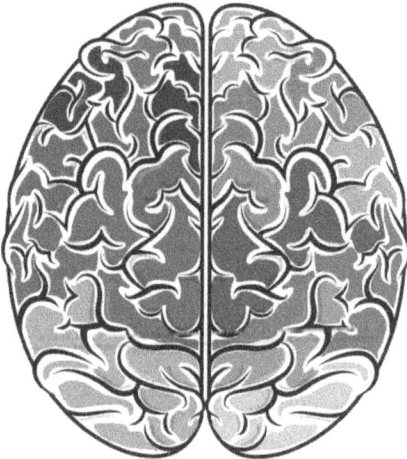

Sheltered Aura

Fight with your heart and mind

Worth it... don't think it's kind

Ask me then my opinion

As crazy as it seems to share to millions!

Bring out your love and deeds

Surface of reflection be your heart

Start another race, right on the mark!

Each being create this sheltered aura

Lighten up those positive fires

As simple as Abracadabra!

Floating Stars

Shouting out from high above

Little shiny stars in their heavenly abode

Some brighter than the rest

Have they failed their ultimate test?

Closer on moving towards these enormous beasts

Gently floating seemingly dead

Life emitting from every atomic pore

Blissful paradise, no more pain to endure!

Were they once us

Humanly clad, walking amongst all?

Reach up then after their passing

To look upon and make us hold strong and tall!

Chriselda Barretto

Bearing

Crying bitterly into his arms

Spread around her, so warm and full of charm

A heath of gentle love anecdote

Only for her he would devote!

Caressing her hair, strands of cotton

Soft and gleaming like a midnight ocean

Sprays of fresh grass filling his air

This was his moment of care!

She lived for this, right here right now

Him be hers forever bound

Time might change the ways around

Yet stay this way, hope in longing

They would always be each other's bearing!

Nightfall

"Must work" said her mind

Thinking aloud would be labelled a crime

Dust strewn all around

A growing feeling of unease

Creeping under her skin, into her bound!

Dusting away till the light shine through

Never enough she had to continue

Sick was her mind, but cure not yet due

Hopeless soul lost amidst it all

Fearful of what others might her call

Had to get it all done before nightfall!

Eroded

Stare on I dare you to

Whilst I do the same too

Seaming on patches of your skin

Spread out oh so thin!

Revealing fingers on beautiful hands

Manicured nails stretched out on strands

Much to behold in my detailed vision

Forming in me thoughts of another erosion!

Golden Balk

Visions of a holistic future

Stretching out my inner existence

Rising up to a feverous pitch

Bringing me to that imperfect slip!

Graduate us now on a fervent dip

Bearing in mind all of the many unseen trips

Keep it whole then, insurmountable clips

Create that rift in an unbelievable rip!

Forsake them not these vicious thoughts

Therein lies all the golden balks

Of history and the restful past

Take this unforgettable new walk!

Nature

Fly on high a summer's breeze

Stirring gently many a green leaves

Ease out dearly that hold of spring

Coming forth nature, the glory it brings!

Inhale the freedom off those precious vines

Blooming petals of the heavenly kind

Smell the pureness, behold the greater mind

Senses captured in a seconded frame

This can't be part of any dreaded game

Bringing sheaths of unconvoluted fame!

Stroke

Dreaming silently, watching aimlessly

Trying to figure you out

Feeling your thoughts work away

Splashes of paint all over you

See it now, that visionary pout!

Move on with your precise strokes

Building momentum with each strike

Vibrating colours on different textures

Fingers mixing in that light!

Can this be my unfaithful hoax?

Healing it is just to watch

You be my one and only match!

It Is...

It's when you hate

That you learn love

It's when you fail

That you know your call

It's when you cry

That you know true joy

It's when you fear

That you realise what's dear!

Chriselda Barretto

Vagabond

Call out to that wild spirit

Ye that knoweth no dwelling

Vagabond on its continued journey

Experience in the gain and making!

Dust out your content from the soul

Immerge into the airy folds

Heading only to the innermost door

The one, the only that comes before!

Time

Tic...toc...I hear that sound

Humming through my head

Personifying the essence of time

Leaving me in and all around!

Grateful then must we be

For the experiences gained whilst we see

One more day, one more minute

This rehearsal of all that is to come

Or is it something of a has-been?

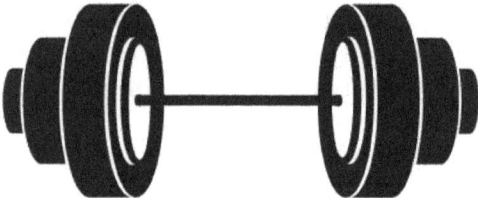

Endure

Tread on carefully dear soul

Started out bitter, but you were whole

Now under-nourishing your mindful scroll

Trending on a different role!

Be it a wonder or a failure

Time approving all of your endeavours

Fear not built in a glitch of a tremor

Yet you seek something much more

The right of a grateful endurer!

Untread Path

Love under a spiral of hates

Joy hidden in each breath of sorrow

Perception increased with dynamic secrecy

Light covered over and again before darkness!

Yield out this undeserved greatness

Sinking in each pore of tameness

For born is he without a stone of dread

Yet endeth we with tons of fear on paths untread!

Excess

Pray tell where lies this cocoon

Amidst many a god forsaken place

Think ye, it might be more than a lyrical boon

No more burdened silence, under one moon?

Give in to that depth of limitless access

Fresh out of a one man's genuine press

Bind it all...hell, havoc on a game of unplayed chess

Mindless fascination leading to a will's excess!

Heirloom

Rushing into superseded freedom

Far away from a crawling hype of wisdom

Rinsing out the heart of the gloomed doom

Extinct it seems on par with an heirloom!

See into the rays of transition

Blinded in colours of unforeseen vision

Senses haywire, full of discriminatory power

Guiding those rest, left in the dirt and fire!

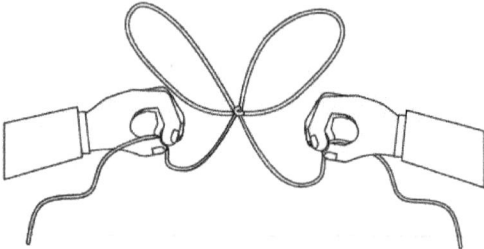

Vigour

Trim out your fears and needs

Leap forward on unknown kilt

Grasp out of that vicious cycle

Bring forth your proclaimed deeds!

Raining out in sheer power

Addictions lost to unequal skelter

No more roof, or a worthysome shelter

Grinding vigour, reap now, this your ever after!

Chirp

Hidden up on that branch so high

Chirping sweet nothings, barely crying

Sending out a notice for all those that seek

Giving them a little feel, from a guided beak!

Down below stands a wretched soul

Knows no more than to bury a hole

Spinning it's eyes, an uneasy feel

Hell damnation, creeping on every inch of heel!

Branch

Hush them, those wailing sounds

Far away, on a once no-man's ground

Surreptitiously uncovering the merging bound

Souls once lost, maybe now found!

See then that curved edge, sharp and protruding

Slithering trails of a luscious mirror

Liquefying paths of cold embodiment

Gracefully striving for the lacking embitterment!

Will thy self to grasp on that branch

Leading to that depth of a cloaked trance

Fathom peaked on a tether

Sight as forgiving as the darkest never!

Twined

Turned inside thy unworthy twines

Hardened woodland of creeping vines

Solace unseen under its affiliated times

Thinking tanks bludgeoned with effortless crimes!

Graphic images of horror and gloom

Pass it away, return ye there seldomly soon

Forget me nots of another era

Building a bridge, over unaccustomed water!

Wayside

Throw away those unseen blues

Hindrances umpteenth on the loose

Gratifyingly sufficient in the very few

Enlightened views, booming with wayside views!

I heard that ripened say

Going on, continue on, be on your way

Similar enclosures, mighty real and affray

Scariest turn then, on earth, it under be overlaid!

Chriselda Barretto

Blush

Blushes so soft like raspberry red

Makes it all easier to thread

Intensifying the woes like ginger on ice

Breathtakingly adorned with this unique spice!

Shiver and shimmer on that bold and brazen blue

To your immaculate condition given to an only few

Seemingly attached to that silver hue

Tread on by that gutsy gold seam

Making it so very live

Intentionally devising the unique grand hive!

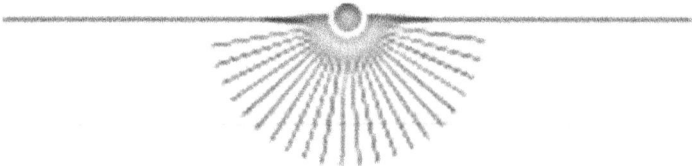

Ley Lines

Guest by day, traveller by night

Wilful and urgent, this trending plight

Sealing a fate too bright to consider

Hampering a vicious, nasty fight!

Yet through comes out a star

Nothing short of a miraculous wonder

Dividing the thoughts creamed with fire

Opening up them ley lines of yonder!

Wafer-Like

Soar on that bright wind

Full of vigour, hard to take on

Snap out of that gracious beam

Reflections of wafer-like sweet breaks of dawn!

Sugar tasted with each swirl of rushing air

Scratching off all that was dead, gladly bare

Next step, just a little bit more

Rising waves of fulfilment on the very snare!

Cotton spread on your palms

Scatter them further, on those lush greens

Vision now lost, burn out your senses

Beauty on your top, above each and every crises!

Suffragette

She cried out of her senses

Sheer despair, beaming at its hinges

Shedding her thoughts and beliefs

Resting in her minds deepest crevices!

With every drop, inching out attached negativity

Spreading thin, creeping riddled sensitivities

Cleansing out the coloured palettes

Years of depressed feministic rights and fates

Blooming on with the beautiful suffragettes!

Dark Pearl

Hinged between despair and hope

You came, you saw, you conquered, to the fore

Chanting on about this never-ending rope

Hanging on to that shred of part-torn!

Glistened dark pearls of wisdom

Enhancing on every score, yet scorned

Blistering rounds of confidence galore

Internally broken, a steel hardened door!

Break thee now...you are brittle

Know you then your existence, sheer riddled

Draft it for you, the winds of change

Surrender thy will, no more the shame!

Splinter

Ride that ghastly tide of doom

Crash against your self-afflicted horror and gloom

Raise out the submerged indecisiveness

Clock on that splintered hope of a bloom!

Wincing out that barred vengeance

Crest once fallen, now standing tall and ablazing

Heaps of courage, boundless and energetic

Forget you that tide

Shimmering softness, offensive movement rapidly failing!

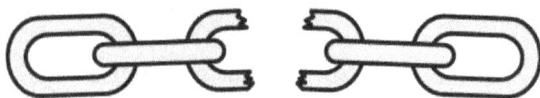

Pre-Set Creed

Feeling the sheer rise of greed

From a minute and sparse seed

Breaking down the rambunctious pre-set creed

To safe guard life, in its mere sheath!

Teaching them the lowest drop

When above it all, was fair crop

Losing sanctity and the will to rock

Was that your plan, from the very lot!

Against the mighty force you stand

Nature be at your very hand

Crush them powered fake strands

This I tell you, claiming my only band!

The Beautified Field

His breath I yearn

His hands, that cold burn

His eyes dissecting my every turn

Locking us in a whirlwind, upturned!

But there is this secret I hide

Kept away on the inside, oh so sly

Jealousy hinging on every try

Keeping you always at my side!

Playing an apt game, to and fro

Hidden pleasure on the beautified field

Bringing all that we ever need, superstitiously freed

Reaching both our inner willed seeds!

Blinder

I heard you whisper, you loved

I felt your heart, cold and curled

I recognised some traits earlier on

Ghastly, yet I preferred the blinders donned!

Giving you up was hard

Long term success, they abhorred

Yet, sorrow I felt for you undue

For changes that took place in you

Life has unfortunately left its mark

Deep ruptured in your being, your heart!

Breach

Inch on that steep hill

Heading right on ahead

Kilter on, reach for that kill

Bracing that dire sheer will!

Render your force uncollectible

Breaching gravity, a mere crucible

Flashing streaks of a world immortal

Strain on, reign in, you are indestructible!

Calleth for all forms immortal

Designed creature immensely frugal

Layeth out a regular eight-dimensional

Ninth on your path duly creational!

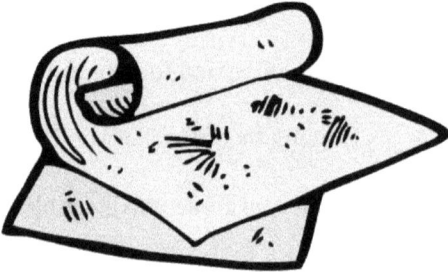

Parched Paper

These words are brilliantly genius

Say them old men of regress

Nitpick them, explore and develop

Till you reach its stupor

Finally finding your vigour!

Written on parched paper

Wrinkled and stained by furore

Attention spaced in each curve

Move and flow smoothed clove

Earnestly trying every grove!

Pain with every stroke

Breeze aside your feedback, now broke

Patience clinging on for hope

Mighty think, of another folk!

Realistic Tissue

Lay them out aligned

Briefly scooping out the strains

Emotion after emotion

Coloured levels of realistic tissue

Branding out the culpable dictation!

Drive out that seed of distraction

Creeping wildly along the trimmed edges

Here you stand for your damnation

Escape far from imagination!

Rescue that air swallowing thee

Mere trickles of contrasting binges

Dig now strong and courageous

You ultimate fate is quite treacherous!

U naltered

Looking on that lonely path

Shrouded darkness leading to an unaltered mark

Is this what's left?

The deadly bitterness of sweet aftermath!

Distant footsteps, nearing each heart beat

Growing louder, this fleeting echo

Nothingness accompanying these feet

Stopped static right in front of me!

Feeling sight, glaring bright

Yet, darkness surrounding free

Instilling a cold shiver

Beginning an uneven still fright!

Dishonest

Living in an age

of dishonesty

Surviving a rage

of pre-occupational hazardry

Collect your thoughts

and reinforce your mental imagery

For this world is the biggest asset

of evolution for humanity!

Untold Wreath

Blistering solitary confinements

Emerging heat of hopelessness

Scorching depth of nothingness

Searing life into deserted vaults!

Cherish left behind at our heels

Divinity only a word at our teeth

Blinding the path under thy feet

Creating heaps of untold wreaths!

Salivate for water be unpreventable

Drying heat over this combustible

Fallout from thy precious bubbled life

Welcome in a world indestructible!

Lottery

Renew them vows

This girl, finally broken free

Non-existent space now at her disposal

Ring in the destined lottery!

Years of tarnished exasperation

Let go of your simplicity

Ride that wave of unbridled loyalty

Discovering there is yet to find and keep

No more losing precious sleep!

Pave your way now

Define your identity, fight on

Redefining the attitude, no more frown

Look out now, she is on the prowl!

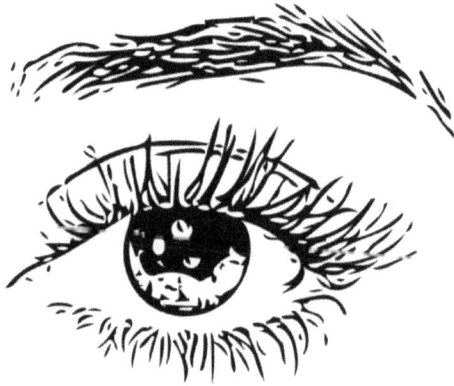

Chasing Eyes!

Your eyes chasing me on

Those irises could burn a storm

Lighten up that retina, dark unknowns

Growing desire, anticipating on its own!

Growl out thy will do serene

Justice and kindness, lost in this scene

Animalistic planes full of cherished dreams

Testing jaggedly, breaking into the worldly beams!

The Quarrel

Bring out those unsolicited claims

Witness in your heart pretentious gains

Blowing worthiness of splendour and gold

Tell me this isn't true or revoltingly untold!

Say ye, thee wise men

Born into the stressful messy den

Unfold thy lids, covered with years of dust

Belong to this song, make no precipitating fuss!

Rush thee now, whistle on four

Turn that wind dial, hush then some more

Terror draw you out of your circle

Enter my square, begin now that ultimate quarrel!

Deprived

Fear reach out thy arms

Suffering amidst the dusky dawns

Supremely hold this vicious fawn

Blooming out of deprivation and brawn!

Imminent destruction, a play on hold

Willing it yet to be on many mysterious souls

Burning anger hidden between folds

Ushering in terror and lingering cold!

Spiteful vengeance your preaching call

Heeding thy need to bring on crushing falls!

Wish no further delay on your behalf

Courage your rival, carve out your staff!

End nearing bitter calls of fire

Seizing all your wisdom of dire

Hither backwards into the pyre!

Lonesome...

In these elicit times of loneliness

When companionship is what you seek!

In these irrevocable times of sadness

When joy and happiness is what you need!

Stuck in the benign middle

This no-man's-land of atrociousness

Feelings up at your pore

Spreading like mist, extreme bitterness!

Tear open that window of light

Dragging me out of this plight

Resurface my addictive fight

Taming once more, my rigid bite!

The Statue And The Tower

Noted for her sobriety

Standing tall in front of all

So long, been there an eternity

Colossal symbol of peace and liberty!

Knowledge and score, in your palms

Leaving out ignorance, making no qualms

Your architecture birthed in France

Yet now on another island you dance!

Made of copper

You neo-classical sculpture

Spread your enlightened philosophy

Breaking the chains, laying under your feet

Roman goddess, your sibling, the tower laid far away

Monumental beings, both visited all year round

High above us all you copiously sway!

Insidious

Beautiful on the inside

Insidious on the prowl

Shade your hunger, even your scowl!

Enlighten them horrific minds

Challenge the questioning trends

Reach the seamless bend

Find you that godforsaken trench!

Deeply emitted with your breath

For they will bury the dead

Never to go unnoticed, take your tread

Beware of the first draft of lead

Seep it out, in your droplet of dread!

Chriselda Barretto

Cataclysmic

Fringe out your evolutionary ideas

They make not revolutionary abhors

Sit and wait for that cataclysmic after

End in sight, or thought you wither

Curse these binging liars

Save them not, drenched in fire

Laughter loud, compassion lost

You be their saviour not, nor host

Grind their minds into the dust

Better serve their purpose

Mixed into this burnt evergreen mud!

Tiny Beak

Sing on with your little chirp

Tiny beak full of hay and dirt

Restless beams of forgetfulness

Leaving with tiny fidgetfullness!

Strike the air on the spur

Reaching heights, only to dare

Beauty amass the chaos down below

Light and swaying hither you to and fro!

Fear holding no bounds for you

Greatness in littleness see we anew

Example you set, now they should follow

Herald on little fellow!

Blunder

Heighten the wind

Deepen the barriers

Already set within

Cringe out the emancipation

Flowering with hope and dissemination!

Hear out the blunders

Reaching out to plunder

Intercept it in full practice

Pragmatism now realised and missed!

Rummage

Grainy images from past lives

Surrounding your head in climbs

Colours in nostalgia buttering out

Those hidden emotional pouts!

Need not go in there, that far

But there lies the key, to your locked afar

Rummage on further, for fear of loss

Integral part of your gloss!

Absence is what you seek

Time enough to rediscover

Plenty sceneries filled all around

Be brave then and step on out!

Unknown

"Ask it from me", he had said

I didn't know that dread

For I had already given to him

My each and every thread!

Stepped away from him, I ran on

Triggering a response not anticipated

Giving now was he, knowing the loss

Of his true support, indeed an intrepid toss!

Time play the judge on our counts

Seek us out from this dredged bound

Come get us both serendipitously

On that midnight train to the unknown

For there will we each other seek and know!

Heart Shaped

This one is for you

You will recognise it

If you are the true, my baby boo!

Your eyes like deep pits

Enriched with years of grandiose soul

Your skin more glowing

Rife with melted chocolate and honey

All of it encouraging me so much more!

Your hands so divine

A pleasure for us, all mankind

But mostly it's your heart

Hidden in depth, but shouting out

Cream-filled, pure, delicate and refined

Honestly spread even, a fine gold-mine

Waiting and ready for me to entwine!

Treaty

Hear me out now

Stop this atrocity foul

Linger on till the end of time

Leeched on in your mind's eye!

Bear witness to this spellbinding treaty

Crease out the differentiation, it is unhealthy

Separation begins at the core

Oil and water, raised up from the ground!

Drenching out this unnatural vile

Becoming one to the everlasting grind!

Censored

Take this punishment

Divulge in its predicament

Engage in this atrocity

Expunge the innate diversity!

Use your censored intuition

To bring forth your courageous determination

Elapsing the circle, holding you down

Sponging you failing crusade

Elliptical orbit of the deeper frown!

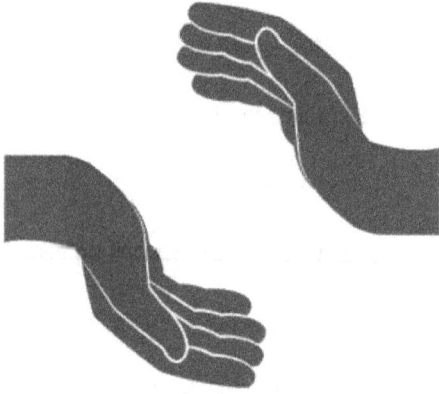

Foreign Notion

You changed my path

Made me doubt my own heart

Splattered my innocent adoration

Made me adopt a completely foreign notion!

Was that your cherished intention?

To confuse and break up my judgement

Loud claps you now hear

No they aren't your peoples cheer

They are shots being fired

Aimed straight at you

Go on then, rush and quickly disappear!

Starving

Opening her purse, in her hand dived

A feeling so gentle, trilled up her spine!

The deeper she dug, the colder it got

Intoxicating fluids, musing up her thoughts!

Behind her it rose, a gigantic Norse

A misty blue haze, difficult to prose

Engulfing the air, thickly and shatteringly gross!

It wanted her being, a test of this species unseen

To carry her away to its eternal has-been

Above the layers of sky, deep above our ground

For his kind were starving, waiting in angst

To feed on this girl, standing tall on her stalks

Crush her they would, over and around their fangs!

Restricted

Open that hindered, restricted view

There stands there, nothing short of a queue

You preference chaining you to the ground

Stand up straight, no hovering around

Blare out you fears

This hidden, deepest mound

Roots of insecurity, spreading

This isn't what they call sound!

Reminiscent waves of hope and light

Driving out those shadowy clouds

Get ready for the mount

Catch that spark, seek your higher ground!

A Simplistic View

A simplistic view of life

Is all it really takes

To keep your worries from going rife

Giving you a meaning at the real life!

Basic is what it is about

No need to push, scream or shout

Emotions running bare, no cages

Run too deep, there is nothing there!

Breathe in this new perfection

Spread it all over, no jurisdiction

Just you, me and all of us in implication

Be the flow, in beautiful supplication!

Shred

Laugh you now, thunder it out

Really was that what it was all about?

Kind and gentle, I am, I was to you

Shredded you me, more than pieces a-two!

Now worry on me, I did good

Blessed am I with a sane peace of mind

Can't speak for you, won't even try

Numbered days ahead, you will die and cry!

Our ways better than ever, now parted

For oil and water, never quite did mix

Neither did good nor bad, an even and right fix!

Segregate

Draw me a blunder

Filler on and around the precipice

Stroke the bright socket

Harshly bending the regret

Watch and wail the segregated play

Hitting far off the end so deep

Begin again now, upcoming laughter

Curse it when you hear the thunder

Crush my dawn, your satisfaction denied

Continued play for the relied

Build it on your dock

Wash away on a tide, sitting on a hammock!

Work-Shed

Wish me well

Look not so deep

Into that horrid, putrid well

Flaming with pride

This superfluous dwell

Hardened as rock

Underneath a sheet of pelt

Rain in on the crust

Wait, sense the brimming dust

Ensnare and protect

Your cosy work-shed

Time pounces on all

Matter your mind, even this fall!

Conundrum

Burst out your conundrums

Crimson in your exuberance

Wine out those salts of Epsom

Cluttering your vivid imagination!

Hidden blessings of superstitions

Craving the cure of betterment

Harden the surface ensnared

Guttering out desires unbundled

Blushing blues of softness

Creeping vales of valued wilderness!

Starve thee in your blistering blood

We that failed, but survived the flood!

Chriselda Barretto

Recreate

Scared are you so, dear?

Of monster and ghouls

Hiding away from it all

With your un-emotive scowl!

Scared are you of the truth?

Fear mounting with every reveal

Created to keep you away

To hide from your enriching living!

Know not fear or fright

Words harbouring more than might

Release the chains of disillusionment

For in there we find gracious fulfilment!

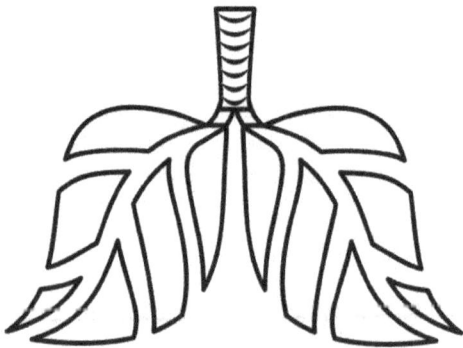

Intensities

Scream atop from your lungs

Exhale out those restrictions

Free up the internal glue

Dissipate, unwind and allow those few

Millions of particles, dust like sand

Gushing out in exceeding intensities

Enraptured embodiment of surrender

Know thee now your beautiful pleasure!

Freed at last, this burdensome endeavour

Take home your instinct

For you are healed, engraved forever!

Cluttered

We are all mere beings

Living off of borrowed time

Holding it vividly together

Falling apart at the seams!

Entire with complexities and fears

Our head exploding from the sheer

Feelings buried, alight from under

Spilling emotions like many blunders!

Personified moments of shrill clutter

Nomenclature and hidden calendars

Each one riding their own cards

In the end for the reveal, held no bars!

Daring

Elegant deception

Bring on the seduction

Throw out the erosion

Filling in sweet suspicion

Daring to discover

Every inch of pure endeavour

Brimming full of high gear

Seeding out the stratosphere!

Pray tell us the secret

You hold in harmony of kindred spirit

Avoiding the gritty path

Onto your next, yet never the last task!

Chriselda Barretto

Middle

Superfluous being

Covering words with honey and cream

Feels like an absolute dream

You burn them all at the seam

When the act brings out a scene!

Say again, repeat if you may

You aren't part of no team

Sitting on that middle beam

Well protected, so it may seem!

Numbered days

Chequered your ways

Set in your highfalutin sways

Inside growing further the decay!

Change is hard for you turgid being

Give it up, this rocky feeling

Most difficult in dealing

Wish you well...a few are willing!

Intelligence Being!

The search has just begun
The find of an intelligent being
To interact with and be part of the scene!
Wishing on a rare kind of star
To humour and bring out the hidden dark!
Waiting for the magnanimous universe
To select, delete, investigate and uncurse!
A graze of good fortune, in much abundance
Droplets of good luck on this prance
Filled with stupendous hope and lit up darts
Giving a firm but gentle nuance!
Worries aside, fear and expectations by the side
Extremely good thoughts and focus in mind
The skies are looking positively clear
Brimming full of my endless cheer!

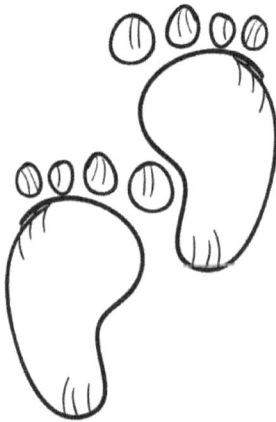

Little Human

Watching this little human play

Bringing back emotions so very rare

Ignoring the world outside

Letting slide the time, so eager to rush by

Exhilarating, ushering in relaxation

Scarce moments of gentle persuasion

Little mini me in the making

Adorable sensations coming in afloating

Carrying away all the worldly cares

Tending to your heart, weaving flares

Summoning enjoyment, hope it forever lasts

To your hearts very own content!

Builders

Tell me what's in your heart

So I don't forget to listen

Show me what's in your mind

So I don't forget to see

Hear my worries and my words

So I don't forget to stay open

See my movements and trials

So I don't forget brilliance

And the importance of expression!

Learn from me, whilst I learn from you

Sharing, caring, building, creating

A future which is so much more strong

Reinforcing and challenging all things anew!

Peek

Standing atop a mountain peak

Below down is a green valley

Now looking so small and bleak

Yet beautiful all around, take a peek!

Lights above shadowed and hued

Covered, then uncovered

The lofty clouds flutter along

Memories come flooding, can't be wrong!

Splendour and cheer on this topped treat

Miles away from the deepest heat

Breezy winds, shivers so slight

Feel a part of this angelical light!

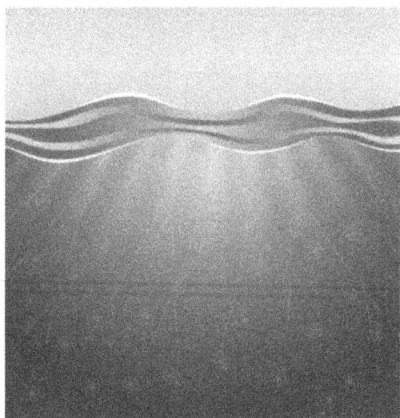

Heavenly Abyss

Into these depths

We creep as one

Scary tunnel of bliss

Drinking in our exhilaration

Hold on, here comes the abyss!

Strongly holding on

Dear being, my only one

Blazing into my eyes

Full of excitement

Ready for our initiation

Moving on gracefully along!

Look at the explosion

Beautiful colours, the truest dawn

Imagination peaked, brightly drawn

We made it, even though not as one!

The Complicity

The complicities of love

Laid bare emotions

Fulfilment of devotion

Enriching dormant dead imagination!

Intricately binding at every pore

Feelings of astonishing galore

Ring in the new, lovely dew

Enlisting joy as one of the many few!

Picture perfect at a glance

Try it then, take a seldom chance

Feel not barred nor battered nor inflicted

Ending may vary, worth it even if restricted!

Promises and vows

Rich in binding thy very now

Open to the merge, souls conflicted

Bear this in mind for when indicted!

Bright Burn

Dream on little girl

Life's not fair, but you will twirl

Twist, climb, run free, never succumb

Knowing in your heart

You will forever brightly burn!

Praise your deeds, superior indeed

Find your will, try till your soul fills

Surrender you never, world might turn over

You will go on, face the rising sun

Bitterly awaiting for your promised jump!

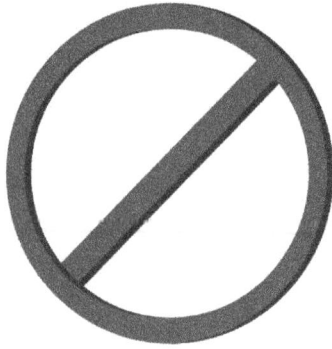

A Piece Of Work!

You are one nasty piece of work

Looking on you truly does hurt

How did you stoop so low?

Didn't life teach you how to simply flow?

Feel sorry for you, so sad and tragic

To stay away is my only clue, my magic

And something I must even need to do!

For you would drag me down with you

An empty place foreign to me, rightly known by you!

Luck to you, all the courage and goodwill

Here breaks our connect understandably

I have yet a steep hill to climb and lots to refill!

Droplets

Little droplet of water

Trailing on your skin

Feeling like a line of fire

Rolling on, never reaching its entire!

Blow it on further

Gently further its racing path

Cooling the surface on impact

Let it not stop, carry it on, let it prosper!

Tingle the effect before it subsides

Moisture lessens, this tiny orb

Reflecting onto its last journey

Now dropping on the floor

Eager to meet earth, submerged divinity

Peace following this enormous escape!

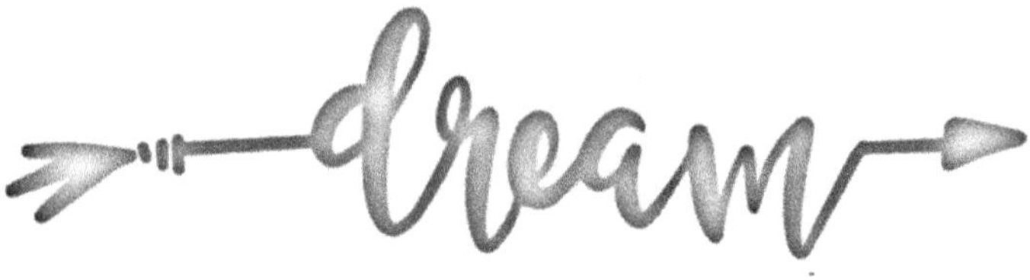
dream

Lofty Dreams

Live out lofty floating dreams

Participate in the other realms

Drive thee under the forces

To find delicate intricate closes

Near the edge of no return

To touch the surface of a higher yearn

Tearing a pull, yet you want more

Sear the thought, then to deliver

Hearty and full, almost seeming like a thin cover!

Swirls

Looking into your eyes
Soft glowing pearls
Against the dark hues of the skies
Tumultuous swirls, dipping in and out
Rounding at the corners, but not so quite
Enchanting the sparkles, bringing forth
Emotional recollections, of the near past
Timeless seams riding on waves
Frothing up at the edge of the shore
Layers of glistening sands
Venturing into the next unified band
Still your heart beats, close your eyes
Breathe in the pale lightness of it all
Withstanding the insurmountable pleasure
Patched up senses, holding a special treasure!

Remember Not To Forget!

Remembering that evening, that minute, that second

When you spoke those harsh words

Ending a ripe beginning, never to mend

The path looked forlorn, dark and steeply bent!

I thought I heard glass shatter

Ahead somewhere, why should I bother?

Only it was precisely my case, my matter

My heart it was, then ready to surrender!

Breathe little girl, it will be fine

What goes around, comes around

Time will pass, heal, maybe she will forgive

Re-engage no way, forget must she never!

Fairy Dust

Cover her in diamonds

Adorn her hair with pearls

Look how they swirl

Creative energy in a wholesome twirl!

Look around the space in bold

Furnishings in silver and deep gold

Fairy dust covering the old

Enchanting, leaving out the cold!

Glitter on her sparkled look

Is that what it took?

Cause everything now means moot

Realise that it costs many mouths food!

Break!

Unchain my soul

Unhook my desire

Unbind this precious fire

Burning my entire!

Unsing your devoted words

Take me on a voyage, leave the dirt

In line with this situational birth

Unsaddled, muddled back on to earth!

Separated and freed

Falling away, into the sheets

No...No.... Hesitation rises deep

Back towards you, I want to leap!

Protect my fall, usher in your call

Chained now, beginning my crawl!

On Hold

It is so very cold

Looking ahead, the air is on hold

I see you walking towards me

Blurry at first, now closer, clearly I see

Warmth in your eyes

Filling my heart

Heat radiating from that smile

Enveloping me in a cosy pile

Your hands take mine

Go on then, richness spreading on contact

You pull me closer

Dare I resist

Closer still, I want no space

Just you, just me, encircled in heat

The cold has disappeared

For now I am enraptured!

Battlefield

Think you know me

Just wait and you will see

Look again, clear your mind free

Remove the mesh, try and seek!

Expected something did you now

Strong I am, against your vow

Bring it on, so full of your know-how

Battle we will, till one will fall!

Dare you think it be me

Surround yourself, for it won't be easy

This battlefield made for us,

Will see it all, rise up to descend

For you know, this was never really the end!

Start reloading, here comes round two

Scared seems you, I said I would pull through!

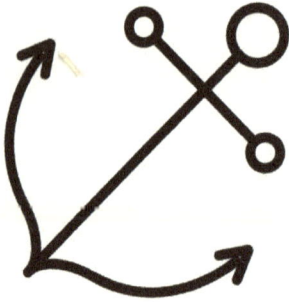

Sprays

Rain on the rivers

Ever so slightly it shimmers

Clashes of blurry vision

Needing no real direction!

Polish the stones

Bring out their colour

Let them dry, into their support

Yield and trash out their inherent torque!

Sprays of water, falling in gushes

Roll on further into the deep unrefined crevices

Blindly following lines of intersection

Intricate its very formation

Earth, wind, sea, all in one personification!

Living In The 21st Century

Can you tell me why:

Someone with no kids

Gives you tips on parenting!

Someone without a committed relationship

Gives you advice on couples therapy!

Someone without grace and elegance

Is promoted to be a role-model!

Someone who is absolutely unfit

Gives you tips on staying fit!

Is this life in the 21st century?

Full of fake-ness and iconicity!

Living in a rose tinted bubble are we?

Half asleep, stuck in the middle it seems

Question, seek, weigh out logically

Find your own truth, be wise, seek true honesty

Research, read, weed out all dishonesty!

Our Dance

Dance with me in the moonlight

Take my hand

Curve my spine with your hand a-slight!

Swirl on the beats

Gently but strong following the feet

Maintain the lines

Forming a whole is what you seek!

Lengthen the step

More complex it will get

Free the spirit

Unleash your regret!

Take this dance further up

See those eyes around you stare

Awe and spellbound, will they dare?

One step to the next

Clear the way, this is a concept

To lead so they follow

Into the depths so hollow!

The Sky Is The Limit

No-one knows your capacity

Only you decide your minutes!

Torch those negations away

Blow out the weeds of dismay

Yield to your inner power

Raging on like the will of a tower

Stand upright, demons fall by the side

For you are your own creator!

Let them that pass you by

Succumb to your intellect and fire

Salute to you all in respect

A weakling no more

A storm in full flow, now all decked!

Love Bubble

So adorable as a flower

Full in bloom and grace

Resisting is futile, there is no power

Bubbles of love, I will on you shower!

This little girl in pink

This beauty, uplifting me whenever I sink

Innocence in all her ways

My child, my inspiration, my silk and lace!

Softer than the faintest cloud

My baby girl, her every cute chatter

Holding on to my little finger

Impressing me time after time with her delightful banter

Cookies and cakes, the sweetest pleasure

Know not one, without my lovely treasure!

Soar

Leave your plans at the door

Step in, only if you want some more

Raise your level, our aim is to soar

Reaching higher, up and above

Internalise and reach the core!

Filling with light, mixed with air

Shred those holds imprisoning your beliefs

Exploding through with strength, might and dare!

No stopping you now

One with universe and the air

Light as a feather, bounce off the clouds

Go on further, this was the first vow!

From Mother To Son...

When I think of the world

Of all I love and cherish

It all stems to that one moment

When I held you, without a single blemish!

Your smile, your eyes, teeny little fingers

Holding on dearly, capturing my thoughts

Blanking out everything, all the love you brought

Dear little thing, never forget

You are my heart

Bound together from the very start!

Addictions

Tell me what's your addiction?
Or free are you from all incapacitations?
Many are there, recognise we just a few
Enhanced feelings of goodness
Reinforcing behaviour, even rewarding
You feel like new!
Seemingly innocent, careful to ignore
High price we pay as a society
Financially even worse in fatality!
Worth not this short term reward
If its end is a lifetime long term way backward!
Find your passion in something else
No better time than now, restart
Many are there: music, knowledge, growth even art!
For you are an important part of a whole
Forget this not, respect yourself, body and soul!

Absolution

Seeking absolution for your deeds

Engraved deeply in your beliefs

Eating up your thoughts, acid frothing in heaps

Seeping deep into the holy seed!

Having tried the ecclesiastical hierarchy

Condemned for all eternity

Salvation not found in conformity

Earth holding no surrender, full of profanity!

Climb up to the skies

Cry out, like thunder in a hundred lashes

Repentance will arrive on scales

Seated surrealistically on the wings of doves

Firmly scathing and healing all surfaces!

Question Freely!

Are we really free?

Left to our own philosophy

Are we truly independent?

Standing tall in our knowledgeable abundance

Could we do and act as we truly feel?

Considering the restrictions, everywhere revealed

Have we got our freedom of thought?

All starting from the same school, we are taught

Do you represent yourself when in speech?

For it comes in a language, scared to breach

What is your perception of freedom?

Could there be a difference of opinion?

Fortress

Stand up strong dear one

Just like me and the other ones!

Life has thrown stuff your way

Now making you a fortress of a different wave!

Deeper still you feel the essence

Required for your true progression

Guiding on to the next conquest

Knowing easy never was it to be

Finally conquering your succession!

Rewards you have always seen

Further down, even on the nastiest paths

So rest assured, take that step

Leading one great effort at a time

Rightful and fight- full, be on your way!

The Dark Alley!

"Come away with me,
Just follow on", he said
My senses tingling with dread
Holding on to my last sane shred!
Up ahead was a dark alley
Leading into fear and folly
Screams echoing from far behind
The sky looking dark and blood red
He turned towards me now
Offering his hand out, for me to hold
Terror rising, fast and utterly bold!
Should I turn and run to flee?
Should I stay, knowing not what will be?
The pleasure of anticipation burning bright
Cares left far behind, in this unholy night!
I grab his palm, stepping into the shadows
Come what may, fear or fright
Hoping earnestly the next few seconds
Will bring me to light!

Atonement In Writing!

Writing away the pain

A beautiful way to stray

Such an innovative way

To get rid of those nasty feelings

Those which would otherwise stay!

Let flow the emotions

Bring out the sentiment

Bleed it onto that parched sheet

Ensuring for you

A manner to delete

All of the remaining sleet!

Need it not only be in writing

It could extend to anything

Painting, singing even simply talking!

Find your positivity, creativity and endearment

Bringing an end to your bereavement

An ultimate atonement!

Afloat

Living for the future

Hoping for the best

Gaining the knowledge

Practicing patience and the rest!

Weaving out your surroundings

Weeding out the non- necessities

Giving in abundance

Appreciating the goodness

Fighting the sorrow

Accepting what was meant to Harrow

Row that boat gently forwards

Stay afloat on this life's barrow!

Moonlight

See the glow

In harmony with its surround

Blaring out with authority

Moving gently with the flow!

Break the spell

Nearly impossible I declare

Mesmerized and hypnotic

Stare on, increase its pull.

This enticing attraction

Centuries commanding on its own

Created to counter-balance

Another great gigantic being

Master never set to be alone

Bringing it home to atone!

Balance it out great forces

Yet a soft spot I feel

Gentler, kinder, cooler still

Spread your light on all our will!

Gentle Wind

Blow on me with gusto

This gentle wind

Moving the scattered leaves

In a circle, all over the bend

The branches sway wild

Sounds beautiful to find

Stirring up my hair

Unsettling it, now in a disarray!

Enchanting smells, flowered perfumes

Baby buds, beauty in bloom

Uplifting all around

Even my spirit

Swaying up and away

Detaching from the ground!

Beat-Nation

Hear the beats

Align your senses

Synchronise the vibrations

Starting at your feet!

Gently raise it higher

Alight each pore

Emotions engaging in galore

Bring in rhythm

Strike at the very core.

Notice your feelings

Utter happiness, never predicted

Pleasure and privilege, deeply inflicted!

Movements follow, engage and focus

Coordination in arms, legs, limbs in whole

Feel no coy or distraction

A level new in elevation

Giving sheer joy and detoxification!

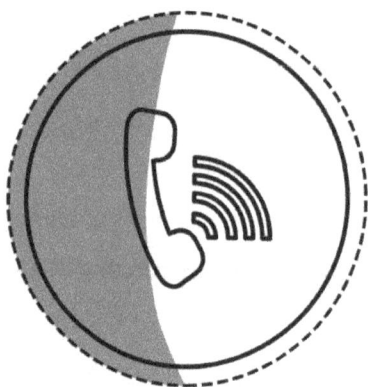

Ghosting

What's Ghosting you ask

Belonging not only to the past

A popular act of our generation

Done it is often and pretty vast

As simple as texting and putting on mask!

Consider it your good luck

Escaping by the trim of your cap

Fault it be not with you

Because reliability and sincerity they lack!

Listen up I will tell you

Better off with the real ones are you

Never to leave you at stake

Stay, fight, defend and live

Here with you now, never to forsake!

Rainbows

Beautiful reality

Touching the sky

In all its glory!

Coloured arches of divinity

Bringing happiness, joy, subtlety!

Watch it, stare even

If you find one

Smile always to follow

Small intricacies of nature

In one's heart to swallow!

Treasure we seek at the end of it

Thinks me, lies it in your mind

Enriching your eyes for your find!

I Am

Am I Daddy's girl or Mummy's doll

I think somewhere in between I fall

Dad's eyes.... Mom's skin

Not to forget, it goes deeper still!

Grandpa and Grandma are in this will

Grandpa's wisdom is a must to mention

Grandma's strength and courage in affliction!

Crazy as it seems in this game of life

Inherit we things of beauty and might

Thankful am I to carry it on my shoulder

Be the bearer, holder and conductor

Knowing some of it will do the next one prouder!

Bricks

Lay em down

The stones of liberation

Brick by brick

Pave us a path

To the dream immaculate

Of achieving freedom

Be it in oppression, mind, belief or simply innate!

The true calling of a mason

Is to build society to a higher niche

Removing barricades, forming bridges

Planting firmly a conviction in belief

Strive will they all, in search of relief

So lead the way, guide and dedicate

The next generation , this be yours to vacate!

Perfection

Living in a Perfectionist Society

Contraire to the innate human philosophy

Living so not in harmony

With nature, self and sobriety!

A change in our mindsets, a need so drastic

For we know it's human to err

Yet expectant are we for correction supreme

Finding fault in things as basic as needs!

Together we shall change the system

Praise faults, because then we learn

Giving need to the human sense of betterment

Climbing and growing will then happen

But first give up we must, over-confidence and perfectionism!

Moderate

Immersion in moderation

Simpler than this, ain't no notion

At the heart of the selection

Is it all about self control and refection!

Add some more thought to it

Eventually you will figure it out

Try as hard as we, remember it's free

And simplifying is better advice indeed

Let's follow up....all of us, you and me!

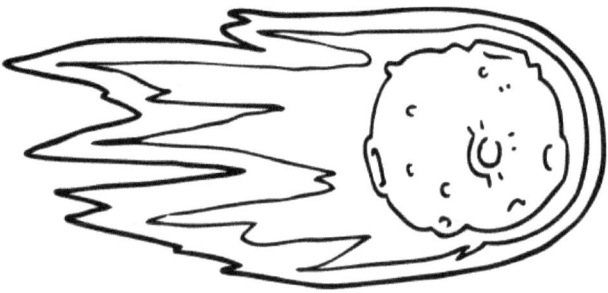

Blazing

One by one

Watch them fall

Gaining speed, before finally hitting

The earth's surface now surrendering.

Craters many all around start forming

Stop now, not really it doesn't!

The second wave now gathering momentum

Stars as huge as planets pouring through

Scary sight for all in this destruction

Blazing trails of fire

Lighting all in its path, till the planet is under

Pray us now for protection

Help us find our way out, our salvation!

Stop And Start

Stop searching, start accepting

Stop procrastinating, start getting it done

Stop acting, start being free

Stop sleep-walking, start waking up

Stop turning to easiness, start facing difficulties

Stop being fake, start being genuine

Stop wasting time, start giving back

Stop materialistic pleasures, start loving nature

Stop talking, start listening

Stop complacency, start proactively

Stop judging, start living!

Grey

Looking out onto the world

This huge grey canvas called the sky

Different shades of grey all around

Bits of blue, blurred and construed.

Levels of degradations

It's like layers of stairs, giving access to other realms

Stepping out of them, I see strange figures

Shadowy and blurry, rubbing my eyes

Sharper my vision, I do see them a many

Coming into our sky to flourish and be happy

Is this called 'Contact', please tell me so

Because frankly I would not know!

Days

Monday

The first day of the week

Feeling feeble and weak

Thoughts of dragging time

Hoping it passed without a beat

Tuesday

So we are stuck in the middle

Having started, now tired a little

Push on through, no don't fiddle

Soon you will see your adult cradle!

Wednesday

We are there half-day

Positivity slowly building

Efficient and making headway

Nothing to stop you, fly up and away

Thursday

Lagging on now,

Motivation needs a gentle *'pow'*

Tell yourself you are nearly there

Search around for your other spare

Friday

Rise and shine brighter

Last day of work, oh wow, all the better

Make your plans easy and undivided

Need to party, so tread on it!

Saturday

The day of Saturn

Rest whole and unturned

Rewind and chill

This should give you a thrill

Sunday

The day of the Sun

To you nothing less than bright

Thoughts of Monday on the horizon

Wish time stopped here, for now and ever!

The Phone Call

He got into his car
by foot, was it too far
the phone call had awoken him
it sounded like his old dad, Jim!
He said to meet him at the station
but his dad was too old to travel
bedridden, always under supervision!
The station was further up the road
he parked and went further afoot
entering this old junction
nobody, not even a reflection!
And then his phone rang again
outside it began to rain
Informed him they of his dad's passing
the head nurse of the aged home, sobbing!
Shock, horror, pain and sadness around him
Now would he truly miss him!

Chriselda Barretto

The Best Recipe

Bake me a cake

would you please for my sake!

Fill it with berries

loads of cherries

add a sprinkle of chocolate

an extra dash of vanilla.

Don't forget the butter

mix in the milk

pour out the batter

Bake it on medium, need not be hotter.

When ready let's eat it together

out in the open, sitting on the grass

watching the bustle around us.

Us sharing our freshly baked cake

feeling joyful, being one with nature

gladly enjoying each other's company and nurture.

What a scenic pleasure, whilst eating our cake,

on our little picnic by the lake!

This Goan Beach

Take a walk on a Goan beach
let your feet eat up the soft sands.
The sun setting over the horizon
feel the heat from it slowly dissipating.
The gentle hues of soft gold and red
tingling in a dash of blue and orange
rendering a superb painting
forever to rest in your eyes and head!
Created by the ensembles of nature
pulling at these nostalgic strings
unawares, hidden in your features.
Create this feeling of utter freedom
let go, relax, feel one with the universe.
Random abstract thoughts
so truly absolute, beautiful and seldom!

Crawler

Crawl on dear fella

find out what's at the next corner

slow, smooth in your tracks

wiggling around, having no clue.

Daylight is your freedom

wide and strewn is your road

no cares or worries, just food,

I long for this freedom too.

Crawl on quickly dear one

cause ahead comes a danger too great

Birds flying high above you

vision better than two of you.

Here he comes now

quick, smooth, light and dainty

scooping you up, into its beak

Oh, dear one, wish you happiness

hope you spent your life truly existent!

Chriselda Barretto

Feelings

Let me feel this

this touch of no expectations

no goals or horizons in sight

just me and the world's plight

Take in zero elements

wishing nothing more of imagination

not even a small figment.

Blank and light

start anew, filling up the board

learning and reliving again

joys of discovery and excitement

like a child stepping into adulthood!

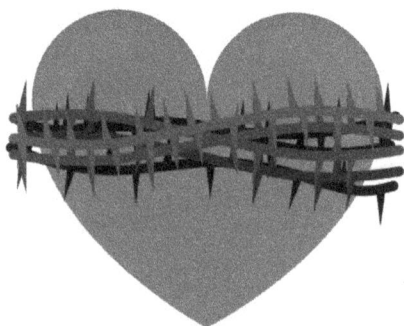

Thorned Heart

Holding my heart in my hand

see it thorned in my palms

Ruby red, eye catching and so uncalm.

Protruding out, I notice the thorns

like little sharp wooden horns.

Removing one, causes an encrustation

of tiny little droplets of diamonds

beautiful and shiny, stunning imagery,

My heart has become a wonder

A work of modernistic art!

See it now in its full glow

enriched with thorns and little diamonds galore,

formations resembling life and its flow

Pathways up, down and so very much more!

Introspection

Measure my thoughts
simplistic and aloft
sometimes rich in depth
to find the key, to introspect.
Memories and imagination
mingling sophistication
dire in need to supersede
every living thought and action.
Bring out the eternal flame
buried under years of tame
discover the find
rediscover your mental blind!
Change and transform
needed to disintegrate and reform.
Clear out and take on the challenge
of beginning again and mending the fringe
Absolutely loving the lofty remains!

Worst

Bring the worst

Why do you insist

on taking me to that bend

bringing out my worst

sad isn't it, in the end?

Wish I luck for you

go ahead strive, work hard

a piece of advice

please don't be you

Be a good soul, stop your play

know it's your time to flay

For in the end we all have a say

in how we spend each passing second

of each and every day!

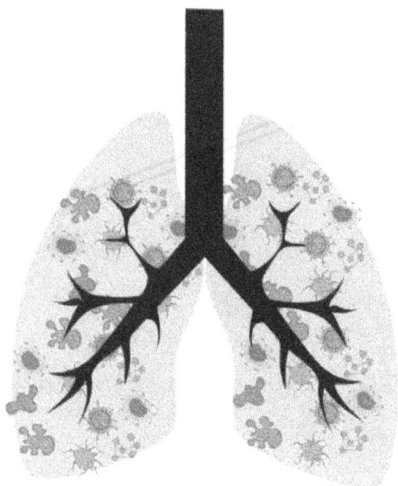

Beautiful Emptiness

Thinking of nothing

pure emptiness

no level of temperature

void of sound

just me, my breaths, my movements

singing my tune without harmony

enjoying it with a certain curiosity

coming to genuine realisation

sometimes it's you to soothe

like only you ever could

initiating a complete change of mood

gradually leaving you calm and renewed!

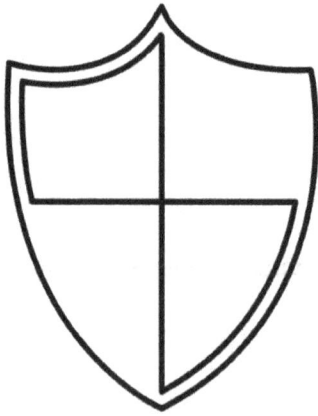

Protect

You are my saviour

my one and only protector

steadying my path

with your daring projector!

Share with me my dream

cause you hold me by the seam

direct me towards your sun

without which I come undone!

Titanic Regretted

Dearest Rose

more beautiful than any English prose

Soft, dainty, pedigreed

fell for Jack one of the lowly.

Adoration on all levels

both minds vying and sincerely connecting.

Hidden paintings for true souls endearing

short-lived but so exciting!

Dear Rose, one regret we see

one question only, I will ask thee.

Had you no place on that log, really?

For then might true love still exist & be!

Airy Gold!

Bedazzle me with your words

airy gold rushing through

warming up my ears

all my senses up and dear!

Lift me higher then

onto much plusher terrain

rich in greens, golds and blues

a feast for my eyesight too!

Never let this end

full of adoration and credence

transformation just at the bend

curing me in all its intense!

Each

Each strand of hair

has a story to tell

be it long, short or in the middle.

Each crust of sand

has seen its times

static or moving with the turbines.

Each person has a life

given at the start to survive

experiences and mindsets forming

with every step and every run

enjoy it all till you reach your last turn!

Endorphins

Watching this rustle

a very gentle bustle

autumn leaves in a puddle

moving free and subtle.

Compare it to a dance

of many million souls

movement synchronised

all in perfect harmony.

Raising our threshold

of peace and serenity

increased levels of non toxicity.

Multiple sets of endorphins

into our minds released.

Feel the success, now go for the win!

Only You!

Thrill seeker,

Adrenaline junkie,

Crazy fella,

Silly immature!

This they tell me of you!

But I see a saint

sometimes a little sinner

then this considerate dreamer

filling my head with sheer pleasure.

Making me reel with laughter,

while in a true gentleman's shoes and then after!

Wish on a star I must have

cause you make me feel in love

all over again, inside out and up and above!

Sentiments increasing, care flowing

another big reason to absolutely go on living!

Blistering

At dusk he arose

to quench his thirst

but something burned his nose

painful blisters now coming forth!

Fear clawing at his senses

he had to awaken from this dream

because the burning he felt now in his knees.

Why him, what had he done?

wish he wouldn't know his outcome.

For he was a player,

a modern day Casanova,

broken so innocent hearts

now his time was carved.

Revenge she swore to take

voodoo she learnt to partake.

He was headed in a very sad state!

The Book Of The Dead

Walking down this long corridor

all alone, darkness looming around

just a good book, I came looking for

millions of books, different widths and colours

in this old state library.

Nothing catches my eyes

continuing on to the next aisle

following the long rail,

reaching the end of the trail.

Out of the shadows, a figure I see

hand towards me, a book on offer

my skin turning cold

wondering who is this being so old!

The grim reaper he was

holding in one hand a book, in the other a scythe!

Suddenly gone, thick dark air around me,

what awaits me next, pain through my head

on the floor I see '*The Book of the Dead*!'

Soul Principles

The principles of the soul

discover them when you feel whole

guiding and leading us all

to the one and only true source!

Curious are we, wonder and awe

yet this feeling isn't at all new

questioned by the enlightened few,

search, research and dawn it will on you!

Connected as one,

headed in that same direction

ways to get there are plenty

see we each other at the end

when it's our moment precise and timely!

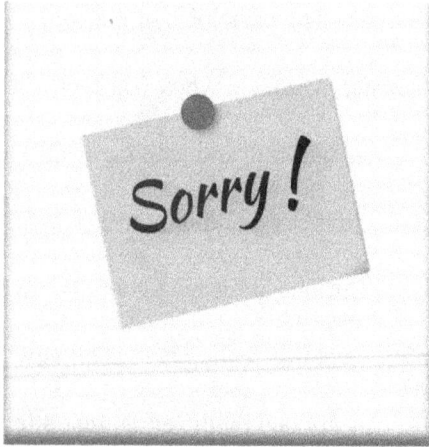

Repent

Repentance a thing of the past

non-existent in our present path

Where hides it at last?

It served as a nice way

to get rid of guilt and those gone astray

keeping simple minds at bay.

No repentance, no salvation!

Free minds are we in daily circulation

Who keeps us in line with respect and compassion?

hope in all this shared freedom

important acts like these

are actually not lost and forgotten!

Just Breathe...

Breathe in the air

penetrating all through you,

your mind, being and soul

releasing you from life's lair!

Positive, fresh, clean, refreshing

ought to be a daily inclination

updating our non-computerised system!

Go forth and spread it through

for we all breathe the same breath,

Our human race on a captivating breakthrough!

Dimensions

Travelling through dimensions

tiring but mind altering.

In and out from one to the next

people aging to and fro,

young to old and back again.

I stay the same, advantageous, a crime?

but that love I miss, time after time

never finding the right prime.

Maybe this wasn't a good idea

on earth be it maybe a lot better.

Who do I dare ask for advice?

cause they are all long goners!

A Beautiful Fix!

Fixing a broken heart

not easy but worth a start.

Take the first step

when you finally decide to move ahead!

Be kind to yourself

know it's ok to ask for help.

Put you to the test

and discover your fighter

stronger than all the rest.

Lastly remember it's all good

this happened to alter your mood.

Clearing up a space just for you.

Better times to come

where happiness will be

your final outcome!

Chriselda Barretto

Humanity

Nature and humanity

two peas in one pod

independently dependant on the other.

One gives, the other takes

reversing roles, forming a joint break.

So strong ones force

destroy the other if in its course!

Finding balance, the in-between

is when these two could shine and gleam

Inconsiderate actions towards the other

mount up the complexity

bringing about only death, decay and the paradoxicality?

The Love Of The Game

Rubies and sapphires

diamonds and all sorts of precious ores

couldn't attract me more

than the love of my score

The love of the game

be it chess, cards, blackjack,

just keep me coming back

to win or be a real sore!

Call up the pals

bring out the cards

lay out the boards

What a fun beginning

to an extremely long evening!

Drinks on display

An oasis for those in thirst

I tend to stay away

For fear of losing focus

And my game winning status!

Urban Jungle

Escape from the urban jungle

Missing the blue skies

tucked above the mountain peaks

The green valley

spread out across the scenery

The grazed pastures

fresh and green,

reflects of the morning sun

The unwinding loop trails

getting lost, not an option.

Here in this rural fairytale landscape

I revisit and blend in

to find my escape

from daily living

in an atrocious urban jungle!

Come away with me, if you may

leave right away, if you just say!

Mind Me

Your mind, a complex being

figure you out, impossible

quite unnerving.

But what's that warmth I feel

deep in my mind

like we've been here before

done this all a long time ago.

Unexplained and unexplored

anticipation building with every score,

simply wanting more, never a bore.

Take this journey one step at every heartbeat

together uncovering this rich and mysterious heath!

This Metaphorical World!

What I see in front of me

is a cloud floating in the deep blue sea

Birds like boats

their wings agile as floats!

Those rays of sunshine

brighten up the surrounding

like when the waves rock through

bringing peace to the imagination!

In this metaphorical world

let me be the mast

of this beautiful ship so vast

wading through wind, storm and dire

reaching the destination I always desire!

ABOUT THE AUTHOR

Chriselda, a multi-genre Author, Blogger and Speaker, with a background in Business Administration and Chemistry/Microbiology lives in Belgium. She is the host of the Podcast - The 3 Pillars!

Having travelled the world extensively, as an In-flight Safety Training Instructor, she has worked in the Aviation industry for nearly two decades.

Always with a touch of artistic creativity along with being a professional modern jazz dancer, she also loves music and is passionate about writing! She is fluent in 5 languages & loves writing poetry, stories, and quotes.

Her writing covers fiction and non-fiction, with the likes of poetry, horror, thriller, romance, supernatural, children's illustration, but she enjoys telling a story in narrative poetry the most! She currently has four WIPs and is also working on her Self-help/Image-Building Book, that she had first started on her blog: 'chriselda.blog'

A qualified Life Coach and Motivational Speaker, she also practices NLP and Mindfulness. Aiming to share her knowledge and experiences, she is a speaker on many topics ranging from Creative writing, Personal Development, Aerotoxic Syndrome to Aviation Safety and Self-Publishing.

CHRISELDA.BLOG

OTHER BOOKS BY THE AUTHOR

STAND-ALONE

SHORTER

DREAMS & DEW

COFFEE & BAGELS

SHE SAID!

ACCURSED FOREST

AVIATION STORIES-1: DYING TO FLY

MELINA'S RAINBOW

THE ULTIMATE COLLECTION OF MILLENNIAL QUOTES

THE CREEP SERIES

THE CREEP-1

THE CREEP REVEALED – 2

www.ingramcontent.com/pod-product-compliance
Lightning Source LLC
Chambersburg PA
CBHW031828090426
42741CB00005B/165